GREAT TALES FROM LONG AGO

THE WOODEN HORSE

Retold by Catherine Storr

Illustrated by Mike Codd

Methuen Children's Books

in association with Belitha Press Ltd.

A LONG TIME AGO, A FIERCE WAR WAS WAGED
by the Kings and Princes of Greece against
King Priam of Troy.
Paris, one of Priam's sons,
had fallen in love with Helen,
the most beautiful woman in the world.
He stole her away from her husband in Sparta,
and carried her back over the dark sea
to the city of Troy.

Copyright © in this format Belitha Press Ltd., 1985
Text copyright © Catherine Storr 1985
Illustrations copyright © Mike Codd 1985
Art Director: Treld Bicknell
First published in Great Britain 1985
by Methuen Children's Books Ltd.,
11 New Fetter Lane, London EC4P 4EE.
Conceived, designed and produced by Belitha Press Ltd.,
2 Beresford Terrace, London N5 2DH.
Printed in Hong Kong by South China Printing Co.
ISBN 0 416 49140 5 (hardback)
ISBN 0 416 49570 2 (paperback)

Note: The story and pictures are based
on *The Iliad* and *The Odyssey*, two long
narrative poems by the blind Greek
poet Homer, and on *The Greek Myths* by
Robert Graves.   c.s.

H ELEN'S HUSBAND, MENELAUS, CALLED ON ALL THE KINGS
and Princes of Greece to go to Troy with him
to demand that Helen should be given back.
If the Trojans would not yield her up,
there would be a war.

The cleverest of all the Greek princes was Odysseus.
He lived on a small rocky island, called Ithaca.
He did not want to go and fight,
so when the messengers came to him,
he pretended to be mad. He ploughed a field with
an ass and an ox yoked together,
and he sowed the earth with salt instead of grain.

To test his madness, one of the messengers
put Odysseus' baby son in front of the yoked animals.
Odysseus did not want to hurt the baby,
so he stopped the plough. Then the messengers knew
that he was only pretending to be mad,
and he had to go with them to Troy.

A PROPHET HAD FORETOLD THAT THE GREEKS
would never conquer Troy
unless the young warrior Achilles fought with them.
Achilles' mother disguised her son as a girl,
so that he should not have to go to war.
She sent him to live with many princesses
in the palace of a king
and no one could tell that he was a boy.
Clever Odysseus laid many gifts of jewels
and embroidered dresses in the King's hall.
Then he ordered soldiers to sound trumpets as if for war.
One of the girls there immediately stripped to the waist
and picked out a shield and a sword
which Odysseus had put with the other gifts.
Then Odysseus knew that this was the warrior, Achilles.

THE TROJANS REFUSED TO GIVE HELEN BACK TO THE GREEKS.
So the war began, and it went on for year after year.
Sometimes the Greeks won a victory,
sometimes the Trojans pushed the Greek army back
towards their black ships on the shore below the city.

The Greek warriors quarrelled between themselves.
Achilles, who was young and proud,
quarrelled with Agamemnon, the greatest Greek king.
Achilles did not want to fight any more.
He threatened to take his own army
and sail away, back to Greece.

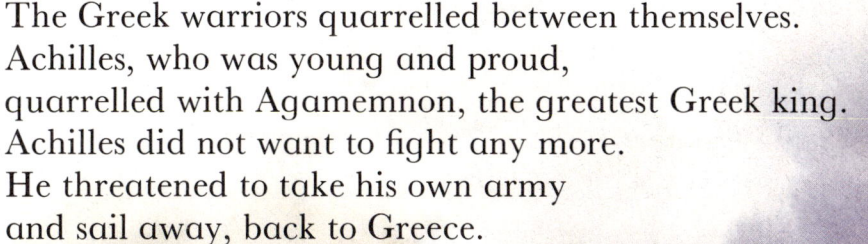

ACHILLES WOULD NOT EVEN GO OUT TO FIGHT HECTOR,
the noblest of the Trojans, and son of King Priam.
Patroclus, Achilles' best friend, went instead,
wearing Achilles' armour. Hector killed him
by thrusting a spear through his body.
Then Achilles was miserable and furious.

He came out of his tent to take his revenge.
He chased Hector round the walls of the city,
and stabbed him in the breast.
Then he dragged Hector's body by the heels
three times round the city.

AFTER THIS THE WAR STILL DRAGGED ON.
Many brave Trojans died and so did many brave Greeks.
Achilles was killed by an arrow, shot by Paris,
the Trojan who loved Helen.

At last Odysseus thought of a cunning plan
by which the city of Troy might be conquered.
He sent messengers to Troy. They said,
"We Greeks are tired of fighting.
We are going to burn our tents
and we shall sail away in our long black ships
for our homes. We have given up the war."

The Trojans looked out from the city walls.
They saw all the tents burning and ships sailing away.
They did not know that the ships had only gone
round a corner out of sight and were waiting there.

On the seashore, the Trojans saw
the statue of a huge horse.

King Priam and his sons went down to the shore,
to look at the huge horse.
They thought that the Greek soldiers had gone for ever,
but that they had left this huge wooden horse
as a present for their goddess, Athene.

Some Trojans wanted to break the horse open
to see what was inside its belly.
Some thought it should be destroyed at once.
King Priam decided that it should be pulled
into the city on rollers.
It was too big to bring in through the city gates
and the wall had to be broken down
in order to draw it into the city.
When it was there, many people came to admire it.
Women gathered flowers
and spread roses round its hooves.

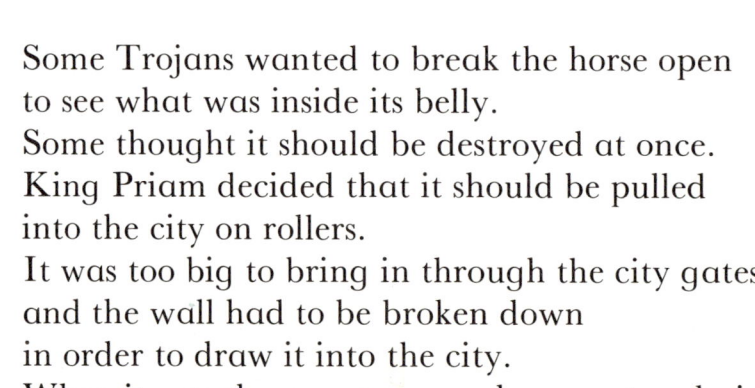

As evening drew on, Helen came out of her palace
to admire the great horse.
As if she had guessed who was hiding inside it,
she called the names of many famous Greek warriors
who were in its belly.
When the Greeks heard her, they wanted to answer,
for Helen imitated the voices of their own wives,
and these men had not seen their wives
for ten weary years.
But they remained silent,
and at last everyone in the city went to sleep.
No soldiers were left to guard the horse,
because the Trojans believed that the danger was over.

I N THE MIDDLE OF THE NIGHT,
from round the rocky corner on the coast,
the long black ships of the Greeks
sailed back to the shore.

Inside the city walls,
something extraordinary was happening to the huge horse.

A door in the horse's belly opened.
A ladder was let down.
Odysseus and the other Greek warriors
climbed down the ladder into the deserted streets of Troy.

The Greeks raced through the streets.
They opened the gates of the city
to the Greek army which was waiting outside.
Then the Greek soldiers ran through the streets
and the palaces and the houses,
killing all the Trojans they could find.

T HE GREEKS STOLE THE TROJAN TREASURES
and took many of the people as slaves.
Menelaus found his wife Helen
and took her back to Sparta.
Then they set fire to the great city of Troy,
and embarked in their long black ships,
to sail back towards Greece.